BUSH NATIVITY

Australia Post

Written by Jo Monie,
Australia Post Philatelic Group

Designed and illustrated by
Marg Towt,
with thanks to Doug Pitt for
his assistance

Production co-ordinated by
Robert Lispet, Sprintpak
Colour separations by Show Ads
Printed by Canberra Press

ISBN 0 642 15516 X

The outback was buzzing
with wonderful news
a wallaby passed it to two kangaroos
spiny echidnas emerged from the ground
busy young bandicoots bounded around
a web-footed platypus gazed at the view
some fluffy-tailed gliders looked longingly too
carolling kookaburras laughed with delight
crimson rosellas sang right through the night

along loped an emu as though in a dream
koalas stopped munching to show their esteem
dancing grey brolgas stepped forward and bowed
bright-crested cockatoos chattered aloud
a possum quite joyfully pricked up one ear
and wide-eyed with wonder a wombat crept near
the stars of the Southern Cross pointed the way
to the Babe who was born on that first Christmas Day.

T

he outback was buzzing
with wonderful news

a wallaby passed it to two kangaroos

S piny echidnas emerged from the ground

busy young bandicoots bounded around

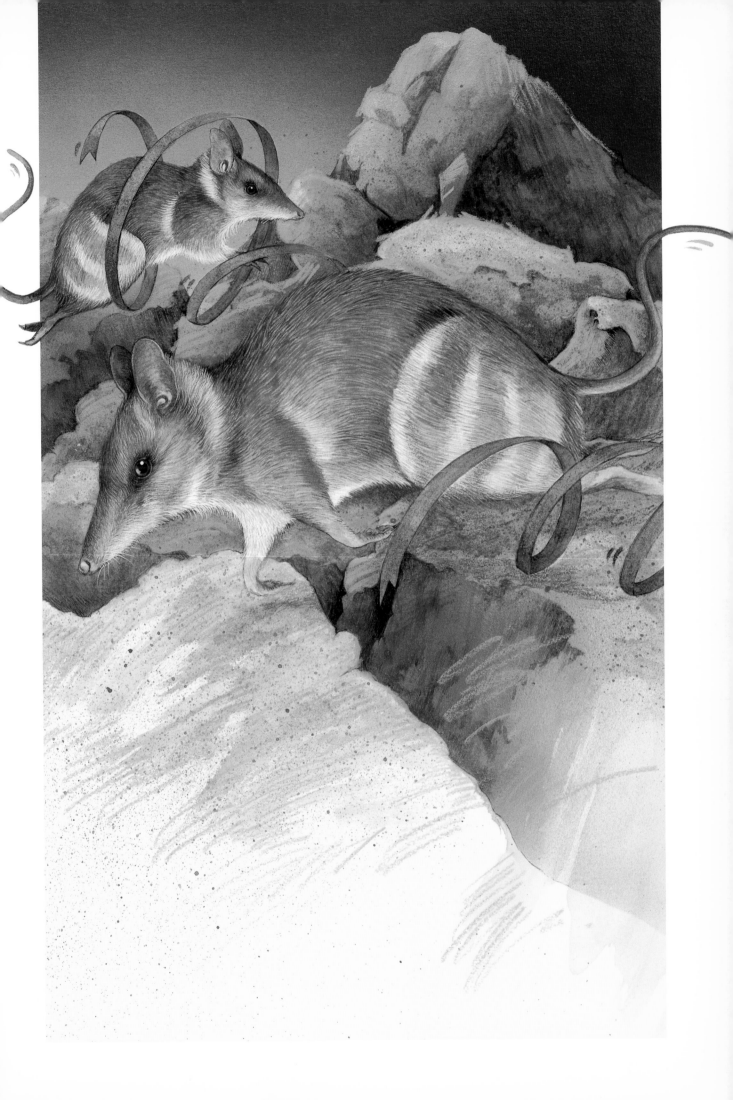

a web-footed platypus
gazed at the view

S ome fluffy-tailed gliders looked longingly too

C arolling kookaburras laughed with delight

C
rimson rosellas
sang right through the night

a

long loped an emu
as though in a dream

k oalas stopped munching to show their esteem

dancing grey brolgas
stepped forward and bowed

bright-crested cockatoos chattered aloud

a

possum quite joyfully
pricked up one ear

and wide-eyed with wonder
a wombat crept near

t he stars of the Southern Cross pointed the way

t o the Babe who was born
on that first Christmas Day.